ONE POTATO, TWO POTATO, THREE POTATO, FOUR

165 Chants for Children

Compiled by Mary Lou Colgin

Designed by Sheila Moceyunas

Previously published as
Chants for Children

gryphon house
Beltsville, Maryland

ONE POTATO, TWO POTATO,
THREE POTATO, FOUR
165 Chants for Children
Compiled by M. L. Colgin
Copyright © 1982 by Mary LOuise N. Colgin
Also publisher of *Chords and Starts for Guitar and Autoharp*, 1980.

Library of Congress Catalog Card Number 88-82376

ISBN 0-87659-141-1

gryphon house
10726 Tucker Street
Beltsville, MD 20705, USA

World Wide Web: http://www.ghbooks.com

Cover illustration copyright© 1988 by Linda Greigg. Inside illustrations used with permission of publisher from Animals by Jim Harter, Dover Publications, Inc., New York, 1979.

Manufactured in the United States of America
First printing July 1982

10   9

Contents

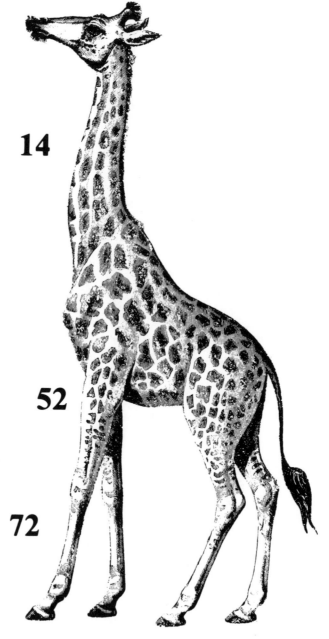

Preface

Language experiences may be the most important element in an early childhood program. Certainly they are of great significance. Chants, or choral speaking, should be included in a host of language activities that help children develop speaking and listening skills prior to learning to read and write.

Ranging from the venerable Mother Goose rhymes to the contemporary jump-rope calls, chants are a kind of word play that can extend both knowledge and vocabulary and provide a sense of language structure. They can serve as a bridge between oral communication and the written word, promoting a love of language and helping to build rapport between adults and children.

Beyond helping to develop listening and speaking skills, stimulating imagination, and aiding memory development, chants are just plain fun. The repetition of sound, rhythms, and patterns can be delightful and challenging.

Chants certainly need not be limited to early childhood programs. Anywhere children gather, including the family, chants are appropriate and enriching.

Sometimes the best chant of all is the child's own creation. Capture it and name it as that child's. People who use *One Potato, Two Potato, Three Potato, Four* will have their own favorites. Note the extra blank pages for chants that spring up from nowhere.

Teach a chant according to what works with and for your children. You may wish to explain it in terms of the children's experiences or the folklore it expresses. Do your children need to hear the chant from you until they "catch" it? Or will repeating it after you line by line be successful? Try a variety of methods. Clap your hands to the rhythm; tap your toes. Get involved and enjoy!

Creatures

Where, oh, where has my little dog gone?
Oh, where, oh, where can he be?
With his tail cut short and his ears cut long,
Oh, where, oh, where can he be?

I never had a dog that could talk
Or a cat that could sing a song
Or a pony that could on two legs walk
And keep it up all the day long.

Or a pig that could whistle a merry tune
Or a hen that could dance a jig
Or a cow that could jump clear over the moon
Or a musical guinea pig.

My little puppy's name is Wags.
He eats so much his tummy sags.
His ears flop-flop and his tail wig-wags;
And when he walks, he walks zig-zags.

Higglety, pigglety, pop!
The dog has eaten the mop.
The pig's in a hurry,
The cat's in a flurry,
Higglety, pigglety, Pop!

1

This little pig went to market,
This little pig stayed home,
This little pig had roast beef,
This little pig had none.
And this little pig cried,
"Wee, wee, wee," all the way home.

What do you see? A pig in a tree.
Where's you cat? Under my hat.
How do you know? He licked my toe.

I had a little pig and fed him in a trough.
He got so fat his tail dropped off.
So I got me a hammer and I got me a nail
And I made my piggie a brand new tail.

Piggy on the railway, picking up some stones;
Along came an engine and broke poor Piggy's bones.

"Oh!" said Piggy, "that's not fair."
"Oh!" said the engine driver, "I don't care!"

2

My old hen's a good old hen.
She lays eggs for sailor men.
Sometimes one, sometimes two.
Sometimes enough for the whole blamed crew.

Cluck, old hen, cluck, I tell you.
Cluck, old hen, or I'm gonna sell you.
Cluck, old hen, cluck, I say.
Cluck, old hen, or I'll give you away.

Chickery, chickery, cranny crow
Went to the well to wash my toe;
When I got back, my chicken was gone.
What'll I do from dusk to dawn?

Chicken in the bread tray, scratching up some dough.
Granny, will your dog bite? No, child, no.

3

Jaybird, jaybird, sitting on a fence,
Trying to make a dollar out of fifteen cents.

Way down yonder a little ways off
A jaybird died from the whooping cough.
He whooped so hard with the whooping cough,
He whooped his head and tail right off.

There was a rat, for want of a stairs,
Went down a rope to say his prayers.

I bought me a hen and my hen loved me;
Fed my hen under yonder tree.
Hen said Fiddle dee dee.

Bought me a turkey and my turkey loved me;
Fed my turkey under yonder tree.
Turkey said Gobble, gobble.
Hen said Fiddle dee dee.

(Others: Cat said meow, meow, etc.)

4

Up in the north a long way off,
A donkey caught the whooping cough.
What shall we give him to make him better?
Salt, mustard, vinegar, and pepper.

Little Arabella Stiller found a wooly caterpillar.
First it crawled up on her mother,
Then up on her baby brother.
All said, "Arabella Stiller, take away that caterpillar."

Bow-wow says the dog
Meow, meow says the cat
Grunt, grunt says the hog
And squeak says the rat.

Tu-whu says the owl
Caw, caw says the crow
Quack, quack goes the duck
And moo says the cow.

The snail is so slow, the snail is so slow.
He creeps and creeps along.
The snail is so-o-o s-l-o-w.

5

Go tell Aunt Rhody,
Go tell Aunt Rhody,
Go tell Aunt Rhody,
The old gray goose is dead.

The one that she was saving,
The one that she was saving,
The one that she was saving
To make a feather bed.

She died on a Friday,
She died on a Friday,
She died on a Friday
Behind the old red shed.

She left nine small goslings,
She left nine small goslings,
She left nine small goslings
To scratch for their own bread.

I never saw a purple cow.
I never hope to see one.
But I can tell you anyhow
I'd rather see than be one.

6

Way down South where bananas grow,
A fly stepped on an elephant's toe.
The elephant cried with tears in his eyes,
"Why don't you pick on someone your own size?"

I asked my mother for fifty cents
To see the elephant jump a fence.
He jumped so high, he reached the sky,
And didn't get down til the Fourth of July.

I asked my mother for fifty more
To see the elephant scrub the floor.
He scrubbed so slow he stubbed his toe,
And that was the end of the elephant show.

Oh, a-hunting we will go, a-hunting we will go!
We'll catch a little fox and put him in a box
And then we'll let him go.

When pussy cat has the gout,
The rats and mice can play about.

Juba this; Juba that;
Juba chased a yellow cat.
Juba up; Juba down;
Juba runnin' all around.

Dormy, dormy, dormouse
Sleeps in his little house.
He won't wake up 'til suppertime,
And that won't be 'til half past nine.

8

Eeny, meeny, miney mo.
Catch a tiger by the toe.
If he hollers, let him go.
Eeny, meeny, miney mo.

I know a little pussy; her coat is silver grey.
She lives down in the meadow not very far away.
Although she is a pussy, she'll never be a cat,
For she's a pussywillow. What do you think of that?
Meow, meow, meow, meow, meow, meow, meow!

9

I know something I won't tell.
Three little monkeys in a peanut shell.
One can read and one can write
And one can smoke a corncob pipe.

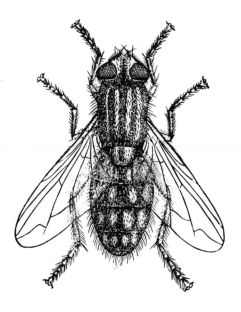

Shoo, fly, don't bother me.
Shoo, fly, don't bother me.
Shoo, fly, don't bother me.
For I belong to somebody.

I feel, I feel, I feel like a morning star.
I feel, I feel, I feel like a morning star.

(Repeat Shoo, fly.)

Old Hogan's goat was feeling fine.
He ate a shirt right off the line.
I took a stick and beat his back
And tied him to a railroad track.

A speeding train was coming nigh.
Old Hogan's goat was doomed to die.
He gave a terrible shriek of pain,
Coughed up that shirt and flagged the train.

Old Dan Tucker went to town
Riding a goat and leading a hound.
The hound gave a yelp and the goat gave a jump
And old Dan Tucker landed on a stump.

Teddy Bear, Teddy Bear, turn all around.
Teddy Bear, Teddy Bear, touch the ground.
Teddy Bear, Teddy Bear, read the news.
Teddy Bear, Teddy Bear, shine your shoes.
Teddy Bear, Teddy Bear, go upstairs.
Teddy Bear, Teddy Bear, say your prayers.
Teddy Bear, Teddy Bear, turn out the light.
Teddy Bear, Teddy Bear, say GOOD NIGHT!

NOTES

NOTES

1
22
333

2, 4, 6, 8, meet me at the garden gate.
If I'm late do not wait, 2, 4, 6, 8.

One, two, buckle my shoe
Three, four, shut the door
Five, six, pick up sticks
Seven, eight, lay them straight
Nine, ten, a good fat hen
Eleven, twelve, dig and delve
Thirteen, fourteen, maids a-courting
Fifteen, sixteen, maids a-milking
Seventeen, eighteen, maids a-waiting
Nineteen, twenty, my plate is empty.

Hippity-hop to the grocery store
To buy three sticks of candy.
One for you and one for me,
And one for sister Mandy.

One, two, three, four,
Mary at the classroom door;
Five, six, seven, eight,
Eating cherries off her plate.

Two little ducks that I once knew,
Fat ones, skinny ones, there were two
But the one little duck with the feathers on his back,
He led the others with a quack, quack, quack.
Down to the river they would go,
Wibble, wobble, wibble, wobble, to and fro.
But the one little duck with the feathers on his back,
He led the others with a quack, quack, quack.
He led the others with a quack, quack, quack.

Five little ducks went swimming one day,
Over the pond and far away.
Mother Duck said, "Quack, quack, quack."
But only four little ducks came back.

Four little ducks . . . three . . . two

One little duck went swimming one day,
Over the pond and far away.
Mother Duck said, "Quack, quack, quack."
And five little ducks came swimming back.

One for the money, two for the show;
Three to get ready, and four to go.

There were five in the bed and the little one said,
"Roll over, Roll over."
So they all rolled over and one fell out — (pause).
There were four in the bed and the little one said,
"Roll over. Roll over."
So they all rolled over and one fell out — (pause).
(Continue with numbers three and two.)
There was one in the bed and the little one said,
"GOOD NIGHT!"

Every morning at eight o'clock
You can hear the mailman's knock.
Up jumps Katy to open the door,
One letter, two letters, three letters,
FOUR.

Five little monkeys, jumping on the bed.
One fell off and bumped his head.
Mama called the doctor, and the doctor said,
"No more monkeys jumping on the bed."

Four little monkeys . . . three . . . two . . . one.

Thirty days hath September,
April, June, and November;
All the rest have thirty one,
Excepting February alone,
And that has twenty eight days clear
And twenty nine in each leap year.

One elephant went out to play
On a spider's web one day.
He had such enormous fun,
He asked another elephant to come

Two elephants went out to play, etc.

Three . . . four . . . etc.

6
7

1 little, 2 little, 3 little kittens (or whatever)
4 little, 5 little, 6 little kittens
7 little, 8 little, 9 little kittens
10 little soft, furry kittens.

(Count backwards for another verse.)

A, B, C, D, E, F, G,
H, I, J, K, L, M, N, O, P,
Q, R, S, T, U, and V,
W, X, Y, and Z.
Now I've said my A, B, C's;
Tell me what you think of me.

ABCD

A, B, C, tumble down D.
The cat's in the cupboard
And can't see me.

ABC's NOTES

NOTES

Food

Peanut, peanut butter — and jelly
Peanut, peanut butter — and jelly
Peanut, peanut butter — and jelly.

First you take a peanut and you smush it,
You smush it.
First you take a peanut and you smush it,
You smush it (Use fist in palm.)

Peanut, peanut butter — and jelly
Peanut, peanut butter — and jelly
Peanut, peanut butter — and jelly.

Then you use a knife to spread it, spread it.
Then you use a knife to spread it, spread it.

Peanut, peanut butter — and jelly
Peanut, peanut butter — and jelly
Peanut, peanut butter — and jelly.

Then you make a sandwich, a sandwich.
Then you make a sandwich, a sandwich.

Peanut, peanut butter — and jelly
Peanut, peanut butter — and jelly
Peanut, peanut butter — and jelly.

THEN YOU EAT IT!

Five little sausages, frying in a pan,
One went pop, and the others went bang!

If I were an apple and grew on a tree,
I think I'd drop down on a nice child like me.
I wouldn't stay there giving nobody joy;
I'd fall down at once and say, "Eat me, my boy."

Handy pandy, Jack-a-dandy,
Loves plum cake and sugar candy.
He bought some at the grocer's shop
And out he came, hop, hop, hop.

Blackberries, blackberries on the hill.
How many pails can you fill?
Briers are thick and briers scratch.
But we'll pick all the berries in the blackberry patch.

A peanut sat on the railroad track
His heart was all a-flutter.
Along came a train — the 5:15 —
Toot, toot, peanut butter.

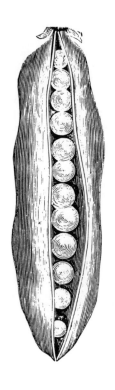

I eat my peas with honey.
I've done it all my life.
It makes the peas taste funny,
But it keeps them on the knife.

Peas porridge hot, peas porridge cold,
Peas porridge in the pot, nine days old.
Some like it hot, some like it cold.
Some like it in the pot, nine days old.

Wake up, Jacob (or any name), day's a-breakin',
Peas in the pot and pancakes bakin',
Bacon's in the pan and coffee's in the pot;
Come on round and get it while it's hot.
(shout) WAKE SNAKES AND BITE A BISCUIT.

I know a little puppy; he hasn't any tail.
He isn't very chubby; he's skinny as a rail.
Although he is a puppy, he'll never be a hound.
They sell him at the shop for 30 cents a pound.
Bow-wow, wow-wow, wow-wow, wow.
HOT DOG!

My father owns the butcher shop,
My mother cuts the meat,
And I'm the little hot dog
That runs around the street.

One potato, two potato,
Three potato, four,
Five potato, six potato,
Seven potato, more.

Doodlebug, doodlebug, come get sweet milk.
Doodlebug, doodlebug, come get some butter.
Doodlebug, doodlebug, come get corn bread.
Doodlebug, doodlebug, come get supper.

There once was a queen whose face was green,
She ate her milk and drank her bread
And got up in the morning to go to bed.

Hot cross buns! Hot cross buns!
One a penny, two a penny.
Hot cross buns!

Soda bread and soft bread
Crazy bread and hard bread
Loaf bread, cornbread
Plain bread and biscuits.

25

Last night, the night before,
A lemon and a pickle came knocking at my door;
I went down to let them in, a-a-and
They hit me on the head with a rolling pin.

The Waffle Man is a fine old man.
He washes his face in a frying pan;
He makes his waffles with his hand.
Everybody loves the Waffle Man.

Jelly on the plate,
Wiggle-waggle, wiggle-waggle,
Jelly on the plate.

Sausage in the pan, sausage in the pan,
Turn it round, turn it round,
Sausage in the pan.

Paper on the floor, paper on the floor,
Pick it up, pick it up,
Paper on the floor.

Baby in the carriage, baby in the carriage,
Pull her out, pull her out,
Baby in the carriage.

*Use this chant as children shake heavy cream
into butter.*

Come, butter, come.
Come, butter, come.
(Child's name)'s at the garden gate
Waiting with banana cake.
Come, butter, come.

NOTES

NOTES

Nursery Rhymes

Old King Cole was a merry old soul
And a merry old soul was he.
He called for his pipe,
And he called for his bowl,
And he called for his fiddlers three.

Hey, diddle, diddle, the cat and the fiddle,
The cow jumped over the moon;
The little dog laughed to see such sport,
And the dish ran away with the spoon.

Old Mother Hubbard went to the cupboard
To get her poor dog a bone;
But when she came there the cupboard was bare,
And so the poor dog had none.

She went to the baker's to buy him some bread,
But when she came back, the poor dog was dead.

She went to the joiner's to buy him a coffin,
But when she came back, the poor dog was laughing.

29

There was a little girl, and she had a little curl
Right in the middle of her forehead.
When she was good, she was very, very good,
But when she was bad, she was horrid.

See-saw, Margery Daw,
Jenny shall have a new master;
She shall have but a penny a day
Because she can't work any faster.

Rock-a-bye, baby, on the tree top.
When the wind blows, the cradle will rock.
When the bough breaks, the cradle will fall,
And down will come baby, cradle, and all.

Bye, baby bunting,
Daddy's gone a-hunting.
Mommy's gone to buy a skin
To rock the baby bunting in.

Sing a song of sixpence, a pocket full of rye;
Four and twenty blackbirds baked in a pie.

When the pie was opened, the birds began to sing;
Wasn't that a dainty dish to set before the king?

The king was in his counting house counting out his money;
The queen was in the parlor eating bread and honey.

The maid was in the garden hanging out the clothes;
Along came a blackbird and pecked her on her nose.

Jack and Jill went up the hill
To fetch a pail of water;
Jack fell down and broke his crown,
And Jill came tumbling after.

The north wind doth blow
And we shall have some snow.
And what will the robin do then, poor thing?
He will sit in the barn and keep himself warm,
With his little head tucked under his wing, poor thing!

To market, to market to buy a fat pig.
Home again, home again, jiggety-jig.
To market, to market to buy a fat hog.
Home again, home again, jiggety-jog.

Tom, Tom, the piper's son,
Stole a pig and away he run;
Pig was eat, and Tom was beat,
And Tom went roaring down the street.

Rub-a-dub-dub, three men in a tub
And who do you think they be?
The butcher, the baker, the candlestick maker,
Turn them out, knaves all three.

Humpty Dumpty sat on a wall,
Humpty Dumpty had a great fall;
All the Kings' horses and all the king's men
Could not put Humpty together again.

Star light, star bright,
First star I've seen tonight.
Wish I may, wish I might
Have the wish I wish tonight.

Hickory, dickory, dock.
The mouse ran up the clock.
The clock struck one,
The mouse ran down.
Hickory, dickory, dock.

Wee Willie Winkie runs through the town,
Upstairs and downstairs in his nightgown.
Rapping at the window, crying through the lock,
"Are the children in their beds?
For it's past eight o'clock!"

The Man in the Moon looked out of the moon,
Looked out of the moon and said,
"Tis time for all children on the earth
To think about getting to bed!"

Twinkle, twinkle, little star,
How I wonder what you are.
Up above the world so high,
Like a diamond in the sky.
Twinkle, twinkle, little star,
How I wonder what you are.

Little Boy Blue, come blow your horn.
The sheep are in the meadow, the cow's in the corn.
But where is the boy who looks after the sheep?
He's under a haystack, fast asleep.

Little Bo-peep has lost her sheep
And can't tell where to find them.
Leave them alone, and they'll come home,
Wagging their tails behind them.

34

Mary had a little lamb,
Its fleece was white as snow.
And everywhere that Mary went,
The lamb was sure to go.

It followed her to school one day,
Which was against the rule.
It made the children laugh and play
To see a lamb at school.

And so the teacher turned it out,
But still it lingered near;
And waited patiently about
'Til Mary did appear.

"What makes the lamb love Mary so?"
The eager children cried.
"Why, Mary loves the lamb, you know,"
The teacher did reply.

Baa, baa, black sheep, have you any wool?
Yes, sir, yes, sir, three bags full;
One for the master, and one for the dame,
And one for the little boy who lives down the lane.

There was an old woman who lived in a shoe.
She had so many children she didn't know what to do.
She gave them some broth, without any bread,
And whipped them all soundly and sent them to bed.

Deedle, deedle, dumpling, my son John
Went to bed with his breeches on.
One shoe off and one shoe on;
Deedle, deedle, dumpling, my son John.

Jack be nimble, Jack be quick,
Jack jump over the candlestick.

Doctor Foster went to Glo'ster
In a shower of rain;
He stepped in a puddle
Up to his middle
And never went there again.

Pussy cat, pussy cat, where have you been?
I've been to London to look at the queen.
Pussy cat, pussy cat, what did you there?
I frightened a little mouse under her chair.

Fee, fi, fo, fum,
I smell the blood of an Englishman.
Be he alive or be he dead,
I'll grind his bones to make me bread.

Polly, put the kettle on,
Polly, put the kettle on,
Polly, put the kettle on;
We'll all have tea.

Sukey, take it off again,
Sukey, take it off again,
Sukey, take it off again;
They've all gone away.

Patty-cake, patty-cake, baker's man;
Bake me a cake as fast as you can.
Pat it and prick it, and mark it with a B,
And put it in the oven for Baby and me.

Jack Sprat could eat no fat,
His wife could eat no lean;
And so betwixt them both, you see,
They licked the platter clean.

Peter, Peter, pumpkin eater,
Had a wife and couldn't keep her.
He put her in a pumpkin shell,
And there he kept her very well.

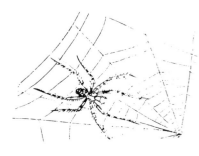

Little Miss Muffet sat on her tuffet,
Eating her curds and whey;
Along came a spider and sat down beside her
And frightened Miss Muffet away.

NOTES

NOTES

People Plus

Stop, look, and listen before you cross the street.
Use your eyes; use your ears; and then use your feet.

I won't go to Macy's anymore, more, more.
There's a big fat policeman at the door, door, door.
He'll take me by the collar, and he'll ask me for a dollar.
So-o-o I won't go to Macy's anymore.

Cinderella, dressed in yellow,
Went uptown with a green umbrella.
She walked so slow she met her beau;
He took her to the picture show.

Here I am, little jumping Joan.
When nobody's with me,
I'm always alone.

Charlie over the ocean,
Charlie over the sea,
Charlie caught a blackbird,
But he can't catch me.

41

Mother, Mother, I am ill;
Call the doctor from over the hill.
In came the doctor, in came the nurse,
In came the lady with the alligator purse.
"Measles," said the doctor.
"Mumps," said the nurse.
"Nothing," said the lady with the alligator purse.

I had a little brother
No bigger than my thumb;
I put him in the coffee pot
Where he rattled like a drum.

Here we go round the mulberry bush,
The mulberry bush, the mulberry bush.
Here we go round the mulberry bush,
So early in the morning.

This is the way we wash our clothes,
Wash our clothes, wash our clothes.
This is the way we wash our clothes,
So early Monday morning.

This is the way we iron our clothes,
Iron our clothes, iron our clothes.
This is the way we iron our clothes,
So early Tuesday morning.

This is the way we scrub our floors,
Scrub our floors, scrub our floors.
This is the way we scrub our floors,
So early Wednesday morning.

This is the way we mend our clothes,
Mend our clothes, mend our clothes.
This is the way we mend our clothes,
So early Thursday morning.

This is the way we bake our bread,
Bake our bread, bake our bread.
This is the way we bake our bread,
So early Friday morning.

This is the way we sweep our house,
Sweep our house, sweep our house.
This is the way we sweep our house,
So early Saturday morning.

This is the way we go to church,
Go to church, go to church.
This is the way we go to church,
So early Sunday morning.

Yankee Doodle came to town,
A-riding on a pony.
He stuck a feather in his cap
And called it Macaroni.

Yankee Doodle, doodle doo,
Yankee doodle dandy
All the lassies are so smart
And sweet as sugar candy.

Oh, the noble Duke of York,
He had ten thousand men;
He led them up to the top of the hill
And he led them down again.

Now, when they were up they were up,
And when they were down they were down.
But when they were only half way up,
They were neither up nor down.

Sam, Sam, the butcher man,
Washed his face in a frying pan,
Combed his hair with a wagon wheel,
And died with a toothache in his heel.

Johnny over the ocean, Johnny over the sea,
Johnny broke a milk bottle and blamed it on me.
I told Ma; Ma told Pa;
Johnny got a whipping and a ha, ha, ha.

44

Cobbler, cobbler, mend my shoe.
Have it done by half past two.
Stitch it up and stitch it down
While I go walking through the town.

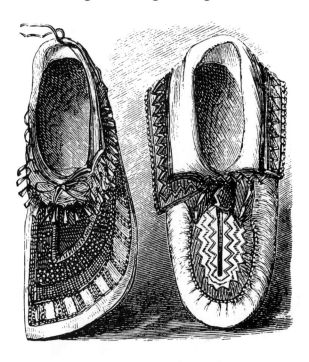

Johnny went to church one day.
He climbed up in the steeple.
He took his shoes and stockings off
And threw them at the people.

I went downtown to fool around.
The policeman shot my britches down.
I asked my mama to sew them up.
She hit me on the coconut.

Down by the station so early in the morning,
See the little puffabillies all in a row.
See the little driver turn the little handle.
Puff, puff; toot, toot; off they go.

Miss Mary Mack, Mack, Mack
All dressed in black, black, black
With silver buttons, buttons, buttons
All down her back, back, back.
She asked her mother, mother mother
For fifteen cents, cents, cents
To see the elephants, elephants, elephants
Jump over the fence, fence, fence.
They jumped so high, high, high
They touched the sky, sky, sky
And they never came down, down, down
'Til the Fourth of July, ly, ly,
And they never came down, down, down
'Til the Fourth of July.

46

Hark! Hark! The dogs do bark!
The beggars are coming to town.
Some in rags and some in tags,
And some in velvet gowns.

"Fire, fire!" said Mrs. McGuire.
"Where, where?" said Mrs. Ware.
"Downtown!" said Mrs. Brown.
"Heaven save us!" said Mrs. Davis.

There was an old man named Finnigan.
He grew a long beard on his chinnigan.
Along came a wind and blew it in again —
Poor old Michael Finnigan.

Queen, Queen Caroline,
Dipped her hair in turpentine;
Turpentine made it shine,
Queen, Queen Caroline.

There was a little boy went into a barn
And lay down on some hay.
An owl came out and flew about,
And the little boy ran away.

Teacher, teacher made a mistake.
She sat down on a chocolate cake.
The cake was soft; teacher fell off.
Teacher, teacher made a mistake.

Smiling girls, rosy boys,
Come and buy my little toys.
Money's made of gingerbread
And sugar horses painted red.

Sally, go round the sun.
Sally, go round the moon.
Sally, go round the chimney pots
On a Sunday afternoon.

Zoom, ba, ba, Mommy's baby
Zoom, ba, ba, Mommy's baby.
Cover her up, pat her on the head.
Give her a little kiss and put her to bed.

What's your name?
    Puddin' 'n' tame.
Ask me again
    And I'll tell you the same.

What's your name?
    Puddin' 'n' tame.
Where do you live?
    In a sieve.

NOTES

NOTES

Holidays and Seasons

Old Mother Witch fell in a ditch,
Picked up a penny,
And thought she was rich.

From ghoulies and ghosties,
Long-legged beasties,
And things that go BUMP in the night,
Good Lord deliver us.

One little, 2 little, 3 little witches (or ghosts, etc.)
Four little, 5 little, 6 little witches,
Seven little, 8 little, 9 little witches,
Ten little witches there.

(Count backwards for another verse.)

Come on in! Get out of your skin
And rattle around in your bones.

Have you seen the ghost of John?
Long white bones and the rest all gone.
Ooh, ooh, ooh, ooh.
Wouldn't we be chilly with no skin on?

Witches, ghosts, and goblins
Witches, ghosts, and goblins
Whoo-o-o-o-o-o
Witches, ghosts, and goblins
Witches, ghosts, and goblins
BOO!

Little Jack Pumpkin Face
Lived on a vine.
Little Jack Pumpkin Face
Thought it was fine.

First he was small and green,
Then big and yellow.
Little Jack Pumpkin Face
Is a fine fellow.

Rain on the green grass
And rain on the tree;
Rain on the housetop
But not on me.

It's raining; it's pouring,
The old man is snoring.
He went to bed with a pain in his head
And didn't get up until morning.

Rain, rain, go away.
Come again some other day.

Rain, rain, go away.
Little Johnny wants to play.

One misty, moisty morning,
When cloudy was the weather,
I met a little old man
Clothed all in leather.

Clothed all in leather,
With a strap under his chin.
And he said, "How do you do?"
And "How do you do?"
And "How do you do?" again.

Frosty weather, snowy weather
When the wind blows,
We all go together.

This is a snowman as round as a ball.
He has two large eyes, but he's not very tall.
If the sun shines down on him today,
My jolly snowman will melt away.

Snow, snow, fly away
Over the hills and far away.

There was a big turkey on a steep green hill
And he said, "Gobble, gobble, gobble, gobble."
His tail spread out like a big feather fan
And he said, "Gobble, gobble, gobble, gobble."

A turkey ran away before Thanksgiving Day.
He said, "They'll make a roast of me if I should stay."
A pumpkin ran away before Thanksgiving Day.
He said, "They'll make a pie of me if I should stay."

Gobble, gobble, gobble
Quack, quack, quack.
A turkey says gobble,
And a duck says quack.

Little Jack Horner sat in a corner
Eating his Christmas pie;
He put in his thumb and pulled out a plum
And said, "What a good boy am I!"

Christmas is coming. The geese are getting fat.
Please to put a penny in an old man's hat.
If you haven't got a penny, a ha'penny will do.
If you haven't got a ha'penny, God bless you.

Jing-a-ling, ling, ling
Jing-a-ling, ling, ling
What a merry tune.
Jing-a-ling, ling, ling
Jing-a-ling, ling, ling
Christmas is coming soon.

57

NOTES

NOTES

Response Chants

These chants may be used as group speech or in the call/response mode or a combination of the two styles. For instance, a leader could chant one line, the group the next line, or half the class respond to the other half. "I went upstairs to make my bed" is a combination of the styles. Or perhaps the group will echo each line, as in "In a dark, dark wood . . ."

There's a big ship sailing on the illy ally oh,
Illy ally oh, illy ally oh.
There's a big ship sailing on the illy ally oh,
Hi, ho, illy ally oh.

There's a big ship sailing, rocking on the sea,
Rocking on the sea, rocking on the sea.
There's a big ship sailing, rocking on the sea,
Hi, ho, rocking on the sea.

There's a big ship sailing back again,
Back again, back again.
There's a big ship sailing back again,
Hi, ho, back again.

A sailor went to sea, sea, sea,
To see what he could see, see, see,
And all that he could see, see, see
Was the bottom of the deep blue sea, sea, sea.

Engine, engine, number nine,
Ring the bell when it's time.
    O—U—T spells out goes he
    Into the middle of the dark blue sea.

Engine, engine, number nine,
Running on Chicago line.
    When she's polished, she will shine.
    Engine, engine, number nine.

Engine, engine, number nine,
Running on Chicago line.
    If the train should jump the track,
    Do you want your money back?

Engine, engine, number nine,
Running on Chicago line.
    See it sparkle, see it shine,
    Engine, engine, number nine.

If the train should jump the track,
Will I get my money back?
    Yes, no, maybe so.

When I was young I had no sense.
I bought a fiddle for 50 cents.
The only tune I could play
Was Over the Hills and Far Away.

So early in the morning
So early in the morning
So early in the morning
Before the break of day.

Who did?
　　Who did?
Who did?
　　Who did?
(Everyone) Who did swallow Jo-jo-jo-jo?

Who did?
　　Who did?
Who did?
　　Who did?
Who did swallow Jo-jo-jo-jo?

Who did?
　　Who did?
Who did?
　　Who did?
Who did swallow Jonah?
　　Who did swallow Jonah?
Who did swallow Jonah down?

Whale did.
　　Whale did.
Whale did.
　　Whale did.
Whale did swallow Jo-jo-jo-jo.
(Repeat this section twice more.)
Whale did swallow Jonah.
　　Whale did swallow Jonah.
Whale did swallow Jonah down.

Gabriel.
    Gabriel.
Gabriel.
    Gabriel.
Gabriel, blow your trump-trump-trump-trump.
(Repeat this section twice more.)
Gabriel, blow your trumpet.
    Gabriel, blow your trumpet.
Gabriel, blow your trumpet loud.

Daniel.
    Daniel.
Daniel.
    Daniel.
Daniel in the li-li-li-li
(Repeat this section twice more.)
Daniel in the lion's
    Daniel in the lion's
Daniel in the lion's den.

Jeremiah, blow the fire
Puff, puff, puff.

I went upstairs.
    Just like me.
I looked in the mirror.
    Just like me.
Saw a little monkey.
    Just like me.

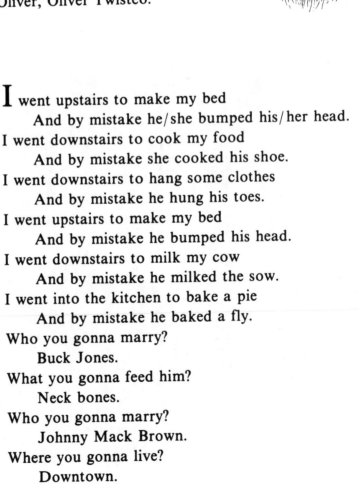

Oliver Twist couldn't do this.
What's the use of trying so?
Give him my toe. Over you go.
Oliver, Oliver Twisteo.

I went upstairs to make my bed
    And by mistake he/she bumped his/her head.
I went downstairs to cook my food
    And by mistake she cooked his shoe.
I went downstairs to hang some clothes
    And by mistake he hung his toes.
I went upstairs to make my bed
    And by mistake he bumped his head.
I went downstairs to milk my cow
    And by mistake he milked the sow.
I went into the kitchen to bake a pie
    And by mistake he baked a fly.
Who you gonna marry?
    Buck Jones.
What you gonna feed him?
    Neck bones.
Who you gonna marry?
    Johnny Mack Brown.
Where you gonna live?
    Downtown.

Did you feed my cow?
    Yes, mam!
Will you tell me how?
    Yes, mam!
What did you feed her?
    Corn and hay.
What did you feed her?
    Corn and hay.

Did you milk her good?
    Yes, mam!
Did you milk her like you should?
    Yes, mam!
How did you milk her?
    Swish, swish, swish!
How did you milk her?
    Swish, swish, swish.

Did my cow get sick?
    Yes, mam!
Was she covered with tick?
    Yes, mam!
Oh, how did she die?
    Uh, uh, uh!
How did she die?
    Uh, uh, uh!

Did the buzzards come?
    Yes, mam!
For to pick her bones?
    Yes, mam!
Oh, how did they come?
    Flap, flap, flap!
How did they come?
    Flap, flap, flap.

65

Oh, I walked around the corner
   And he walked around the block.
And I walked right into a baker's shop
   And he picked up a doughnut
And I wiped off the grease
   And handed the lady a five-cent piece.

Oh, she looked at the nickel
And she looked at me, and she said,
   "Kind sir, can't you plainly see?
   There's a hole in the nickel.
   There's a hole right through!"
Says I, "There's a hole in this doughnut, too!"

Hambone, Hambone, where you been?
   Round the world and I'm going again.
Hambone, Hambone, where's your wife?
   In the kitchen cooking rice.
Hambone, Hambone, have you heard?
Papa's gonna buy you a diamond ring.
   And if that diamond ring don't shine?
Papa's gonna buy you a streetcar line.
   And if that streetcar line get broke?
Papa's gonna buy you a stack of hay.
   And if that stack of hay burn down?
Papa's gonna buy you a wedding gown.
   And if that wedding gown gets torn?
Papa's gonna kick you out the door.
(Everybody) HAMBONE!

Auntie, will your dog bite?
    No, child, no!
Chicken in the bread tray,
    Making up dough.

Auntie, will your broom hit?
    Yes, child, pop!
Chicken in the bread tray,
    Flop! Flop! Flop!

Auntie, will your oven bake?
    Yes, just try!
What's that chicken good for?
    Pie! Pie! Pie!

Auntie, is your pie good?
    Good as you can expect!
Chicken in the bread tray,
    Peck! Peck! Peck!

67

This is often done with one person saying a line, with everyone repeating it in a ghostly voice.

In a dark, dark wood, there was a dark, dark house.
And in that dark, dark house, there was a dark, dark room.
And in that dark, dark room, there was a dark, dark closet.
And in that dark, dark closet, there was a dark, dark shelf.
And in the dark, dark shelf, there was a dark, dark box.
And in that dark, dark box, there was a GHOST!

Who stole the cookies from the cookie jar?
    (Name) stole the cookies from the cookie jar.
Who, me?
    Yes, you.
Couldn't be.
    Then who?

(Another child's name) stole the cookies from the cookie jar.
    Who, me?
Yes, you.
    Couldn't be.
Then who?

(Repeat, using each child's name.)

Let's go on a bear hunt! *(Slap hands on your knees to make a walking noise.)*
Oh, look! I see a wheat field. Can't go around it. Can't go under it.
Have to go through it. All right! Let's go.
(Make hands push aside the wheat. Return to walking.)

Oh, look! I see a river. Can't go around it. Can't go over it.
Have to go through it. All right. Let's go.
(Pretend to swim and then return to walk.)

Oh, look! I see a bridge. Can't go around it. Can't go under it.
Have to walk across it. All right! Let's go.
(Pound chest and then return to walk.)

Oh, look! I see some mud. Can't go around it. Can't go under it.
Have to go through it. All right! Let's go!
(Make sucking noise with cupped hands and return to walk.)

Oh, look! I see a cave. It's a big cave. Let's go inside. All right! Let's go.
(Close eyes and put hands out in front.)
It's dark in here! I feel something! It's furry! Oh, oh! It's a bear! RUN!
(Slap knees fast and loud, not saying anything but going back through the motions.)

I'm tired of running. I'm going to climb a tree to see if we are safe.
(Pretend to climb and look.)
I see him coming! Better climb down and run again!
(Pretend to climb down and slap knees again, run through the wheat field into the cabin and shut the door.)
WHEW! We're home safe!

69

NOTES

NOTES

Index of First Lines

Bibliography

Brewster, Paul G. *Children's Games and Rhymes.* New York: Arno Press, 1976.

Burroughs, Margaret, *Did You Feed My Cow? Street Games, Chants and Rhymes.* Chicago and New York: Follett Publishing Co., 1969.

Daiken, Leslie. *Children's Games Throughout the Year.* New York: Arno Press, 1976.

deAngeli, Marguerite. *A Book of Nursery and Mother Goose Rhymes.* New York: Doubleday & Co., 1954.

Hillary, Mable and Hall, Patricia. *A Guide to the Use of Street/Folk/Musical Games in the Classroom.* Volume II. New York: Interdependent Learning Model, Fordham University, 1976.

Ireson, Barbara. *The Faber Book of Nursery Stories.* Central Islip, NY: Transatlantic, 1967.

Lee, Dennis. *Alligator Pie.* Boston: Houghton Mifflin Co., 1975.

_____ . *Nicholas Knock and Other People.* Boston: Houghton Mifflin Co., 1974.

Lobel, Arnold. *Gregory Griggs and Other Nursery Rhyme People.* New York: Greenwillow Books, 1978.

Morrison, Lillian. *Touch Blue.* New York: Crowell, 1958.

_____ . *A Diller, A Dollar.* New York: Crowell, 1955.

Opie, Iona and Opie, Peter. *The Oxford Nursery Rhyme Book.* London: Oxford University, 1955.

Skolnik, Peter L. *Jump Rope.* New York: Workman Publishing Co., 1974.

Tucker, Nicholas. *Mother Goose Abroad.* New York: Crowell, 1975.

Watson, Clyde. *Catch Me and Kiss Me and Say It Again.* New York: Philomel, 1978.

_____ . *Father Fox's Pennyrhymes.* New York: Crowell, 1971.

Chords and Starts
for Guitar and Autoharp
by Mary Lou Colgin

Nursery Rhymes

Folk

Fun & Game Songs

Holiday

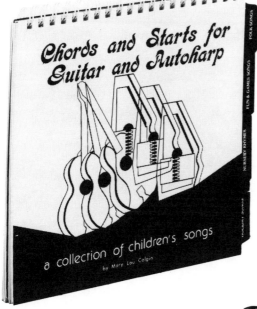

The Only Stand-Up Flip-Chart
Collection of 71 Lyrics for Children:

- Compiled and arranged by early childhood educator
- Sturdy stand-up back cover
- Tabbed dividers
- Starting notes in margin
- Chord changes above words
- Large type
- Appropriate tonal range
- Extra blank pages
- 7 ½-inch size

Move Over, Mother Goose
Finger Plays, Action Verses, and Funny Rhymes
by Ruth I. Dowell

These lively rhymes can be used as both finger plays and action verses. Children can do the finger plays at quiet times and in limited spaces. When used as action verses, they provide an opportunity for energetic movement, either indoors or out. These are verses children want to hear again and again.

The finger plays, action verses and funny rhymes are divided into subject areas including:

- Animals Far and Wide
- Animals Nearby
- Fun and Games
- Colors and Numbers
- Home and Family
- People and Places
- Seasons and Holidays
- Cooking and Eating